GOULD'S

Exotic Birds

THE VICTORIA AND ALBERT
NATURAL HISTORY ILLUSTRATORS

GOULD'S
Exotic Birds

HARRY N. ABRAMS, INC., PUBLISHERS

NEW YORK

Library of Congress Catalog
Card Number: 87-72111
ISBN 0-8109-1029-2

Copyright © 1987 Webb & Bower (Publishers) Limited, Exeter and
The Trustees of the Victoria and Albert Museum, London.

Design by williams and phoa
Production by Nick Facer/Rob Kendrew
Published in 1988 by Harry N. Abrams, Incorporated, New York
A Times Mirror Company
Printed and bound in Spain
D. L. TO 1461 1987

Cover
Western Swallow-tail *Eupetomena hirundo* lithograph by
J Gould and W Hart from the *Supplement to the Trochilidae,
or family of humming-birds (1880-87)*

INTRODUCTION

ohn Gould's life was a quest to learn all he could about birds. For over fifty years, in the mid-nineteenth century, he published a monumental series of bird books, with nearly three thousand illustrations describing birds of every continent except Africa. A man of untiring energy, determination, and business skill, he achieved this phenomenal output by organizing a team of skilful artists, lithographers, printers and colourists. Although primarily a 'closet' ornithologist, describing birds from his enormous collection of stuffed specimens, he was a pioneer in Australian ornithology, discovering many new species during his travels there in 1838-40. The Victorian era was a period of great interest in exploration and natural history discoveries. Visitors flocked to the Zoological Gardens in London to see the latest unusual arrivals, and in 1851 about 75,000 people saw Gould's display of humming-bird specimens. The Victorians were fascinated by shimmering, brightly coloured plumage, and exotic bird feathers were in great demand for fashionable trimmings. Although Gould himself was an avid collector of bird skins he denounced wanton killing and pleaded for the preservation of endangered species. Two years after his death some ladies formed a group for the protection of birds which led to the foundation of modern conservation societies. John Gould was born in Lyme Regis, Dorset, in 1804, but his childhood was spent in the Surrey countryside at Stoke Hill, near Guildford. In 1818, his father was appointed gardener at Windsor Royal Park, and Gould aged fourteen began to learn the same trade. Gould may have seen his first exotic birds and animals at the Royal

JOHN GOULD AT THE AGE OF 45.

LITHOGRAPH BY T.H. MAGUIRE, 1849.

FROM A SERIES OF PORTRAITS OF

DISTINGUISHED SCIENTIFIC MEN

PUBLISHED BY GEORGE RANSOME FOR

THE IPSWICH MUSEUM.

ELIZABETH GOULD, NEE COXEN,

1804-1841. OIL PORTRAIT BY UNKNOWN

ARTIST, PAINTED AFTER HER DEATH,

AGED ONLY 37, HOLDING AN

AUSTRALIAN COCKATIEL, A FAMILY

PET BROUGHT FROM AUSTRALIA.

Menagerie in the park at Sandpit Gate. In his spare time, Gould practised taxidermy (the art of preserving and mounting skins in a lifelike manner), and traded stuffed birds and blown eggs to the young gentlemen at Eton College. He continued his gardener's training for a short time at Ripley Castle, Yorkshire, but in 1825 settled in London as a taxidermist. There was an increasing demand for taxidermy in the nineteenth century as owners of menageries wished to have their creatures preserved, and Victorian 'shades' and cases of elaborate displays became popular. Earlier skins dried or immersed in alcohol had decayed or been eaten by insects, until arsenic soaps were introduced in the 1820s. (An exception is the stuffed grey African parrot of the Duchess of Richmond, Charles II's mistress, who died in 1702, which lies in Westminster Abbey's cool crypt beside the wax effigy of its owner.) John Gould's expertise soon brought royal commissions; he preserved two deer and an ostrich for George IV in 1826, and in 1830 was paid £148 10s for stuffing a giraffe, a crane and two lemurs. As 'Curator and Preserver' at the new Zoological Society Museum in Bruton Street, London, from 1827 to 1838 he looked after stuffed specimens and an aviary which housed live birds while the site at Regent's Park was being prepared. Parrots have been favourite pets since Roman times – the poet Ovid wrote an elegy on Corinna's dead pet, and the great naturalist Carl Linnaeus had a talking parrot which would sit on his shoulder; and tell him when it was lunch-time. Parrots have been beautiful artistic props for portrait painters – Sir Joshua Reynolds had a favourite red macaw which has a prominent place in 'Lady Cockburn and her children'. The child Anne Russell, daughter of the first Duke of Bedford, is portrayed in about 1680 at Woburn Abbey caressing a large crested cockatoo which must have come from the Dutch East Indies. Queen Victoria's pet red macaw 'Lorey' was painted several times by

Sir Edwin Landseer and georgeous birds have featured in the paintings of Tiepolo, Van Dyck and Bonnington. In spite of their artistic potential the first book of parrots, which attempted to show all the parrots then known, was not begun until 1830 by Edward Lear, then only eighteen years old, who later became famous for his nonsense rhymes. Edward Lear

EDWARD LEAR DRAWN IN ROME AT THE AGE OF 28 BY A DANISH ARTIST FRIEND, WILHELM MARSTRAND.

National Portrait Gallery

(1812-88) had an unhappy childhood as the twentieth of twenty-one children (many of whom died in infancy). He was neglected by his mother and looked after by elder sisters. Suffering from asthma and epilepsy he had little formal schooling but as a child copied the birds and animals from Buffon's *Histoire Naturelle* in his father's library. Family financial losses caused him at fifteen to seek hack work colouring screens and fans and making medical drawings of diseases. In 1830 he began drawing birds at the Zoological Society and met the young curator John Gould. Lear used the new process of lithography for the *Illustration of the Family of Psittacidae, or Parrots* (1830-32), a

PENCIL SKETCH WITH INSTRUCTIONS

BY JOHN GOULD SHOWING THE

POSITIONING OF BIRDS FOR AN

UNIDENTIFIED PRINT. GOULD

EMPLOYED PROFESSIONAL ARTISTS

FOR THE FINISHED WORK BUT

PROVIDED THE INITIAL INSPIRATION

BY QUICK LIVELY DRAWINGS.

method of making prints from drawings on prepared stones. Lithographs looked much like printed drawings and had the advantage that they did not require the technical skills of cutting and engraving into wood or metal. To make the prints Lear made outline drawings of the birds on prepared stones with greasy lithographic chalks and pencils, capturing the texture of soft feathers by gentle shading. The drawn stones were then taken to the studio of the lithographic printer Charles Hullmandel. The stones were treated with weak acid and gum, and dampened; then when special black ink was applied it adhered to the drawing and not to the wet stone. Prints were made by passing the stones through a lithographic press and these were hand-coloured by colourists using Lear's richly painted watercolour studies as guides. Lear did not complete his book of parrots, which were almost all drawn from living birds. He found difficulty in persuading his 175 subscribers to pay enough for him to cover the costs of printing and colouring. His rooms were so overflowing with parrot prints that he wrote to a friend that there was no room for visitors except to sit in the grate! In the same year, 1830, Gould planned his first book *A Century of Birds from the Himalayan Mountains* (1830-33) in a similar format and with lithographs printed by Hullmandel. His artistic wife Elizabeth Gould (1804-41) made delicate watercolour studies, guided by her husband's rough drawings, of some unusual birds which he had skilfully stuffed and mounted on perches. She rather laboriously drew the birds on the lithographic stone, finding difficulty in coping with their varied sizes (her original drawing for the Indian magpie *Pica erythrorhyncha (Plate 2)* has the tail falling off the page), and tried hard to make the birds look real and not stuffed. George Edwards, author of *A Book of Uncommon Birds* (1743-51) had attempted to solve this problem in his 'Golden Thrush from Bengal' *(Plate 7)*, by painting an imaginary but unbelievable Indian landscape. Edward Lear assisted Elizabeth Gould, and probably helped her learn to draw the props of foliage and boughs which she later depicted so competently in her illustration of the Quetzal *Trogon resplendens (Plate 14)*. Nicholas Vigors, secretary of the Zoological Society, classified the birds, naming a little sun-bird *Cinnyris Gouldiae (Plate 20)*, after Elizabeth Gould; many years later it was illustrated a second time in Gould's *Birds of Asia.* Gould achieved financial success by organizing a subscription list compiled of illustrious names; by 1866 he had over one thousand subscribers including twelve monarchs. The prints were issued in parts of between four and twenty plates per folder and the subscribers were expected to pay on delivery or annually until the work was completed. This could take a long time; for example *Birds of Asia* (1849-83) was published over a protracted period of thirty-three years! The books were expensive; the 600 plates of *The Birds of Australia* (1840-48) cost £115 and were issued in thirty-six parts which the owner was instructed to bind at his own expense in seven volumes. Monographs of brightly coloured Toucans (1833-35) and Trogons (1835-38) followed the Himalayan birds. An unusual print was of the Quetzal *Trogon resplendens*

(Plate 14) which had such a resplendent long tail that a double folded page was needed to accommodate it. 🕊 In 1838 the Goulds travelled to Australia and spent two years in Tasmania, New South Wales, and South Australia. Gould searched for 'novelties' and was amazed by the beauty of the parakeets and honeyeaters, the 'curious habits' of the bower birds and the lyre bird's elaborate display of its tail. He saw flocks of green budgerigars, or grass parakeets *Melopsittacus undulatus*, and brought two back to England, which became favourite pets and the ancestors of the budgerigar cage-birds so popular throughout the world. Tragically, in 1841, a year after their return, Elizabeth Gould died, aged thirty-seven, after the birth of her sixth surviving child. A posthumous painting shows her with a pet cockatiel from Australia. She illustrated a pair of these in *Birds of Australia* based on Edward Lear's lithograph of two live birds *Nymphicus hollandicus (Plate 9)*, belonging to the Countess of Mountcharles. 🕊 After Elizabeth Gould's death, Gould's artist for the *Monograph of the Humming-Birds* (1849-61) was Henry Constantine Richter (1821-1902). He illustrated the books from Gould's collection of over one thousand stuffed humming-birds. These were displayed suspended by wires and amongst dried greenery, in specially designed hexagonal cases, at a pavilion in the Zoological Gardens and were described as 'feathered jewels glittering in our vision' by Charles Dickens (*Household Notes*, June 1851). It was in Philadelphia at Bartram's Gardens that Gould saw his first live 'hummer' in 1857, when his "earnest day-thoughts and not infrequent

night-dreams of thirty years" were realized by the sight of a single ruby-throated humming-bird. A few days later at the Capitol Gardens in Washington, Gould was gratified by the sight of from fifty to sixty in a single tree. Although Gould's illustration of the ruby-throated humming-bird *Trochilus colubris (Plate 26)*, is a faithful picture of this species, Gould's experience of seeing a mass of these tiny birds is better captured by the American naturalist J. J. Audubon (1785-1851). His double-elephant sized aquatints in *Birds of America* (1827-38) depicted dramatically their moth-like agility. In America, Gould tried to keep a humming-bird in captivity; he travelled with one suspended to a button of his coat "in a little thin gauzy bag distended by a piece of whale bone", and fed it with saccharine fluid which it could pump out of a little bottle. Unfortunately, two humming-birds which Gould bought back to England soon died. ✦ Many experiments were made by Gould's colourists with varnished colours over gold leaf to try to capture the humming-bird's iridescence and at the Great Exhibition of 1851 a demonstration showed Gould's invention of a new method of luminous and metallic colouring used in his books. Over 300 plates in the *Monograph of the Humming-Birds* reveal their variety from the bijou Helena's Calypte, the Shining Sunbeam (Gould's favourite) with its luminous purplish-crimson back, the brilliant Fiery Topaz and the extraordinary

Helmet Crest, to the larger Chimborazian Hill Star which lives near the snow-line of the Andes *(Plates 29, 30, 21, 31 and 22)*. The splendid *Birds of New Guinea* (1875-88) was Gould's final series, completed by Dr Bowdler Sharpe. William Matthew Hart (1830-1908) illustrated the beautiful cockatoos, Fruit-pigeons, a purple and violet Manucode and superb birds of paradise with rich colours and often elaborate landscape settings. Hart had a large family to support and lived in south-east London with little means, and so never saw in the wild the birds he depicted so imaginatively. Apart from the yellow Papuan Bird of Paradise *Paradisea papuana (Plate 34)* which arrived at the Zoo in 1862, the birds of paradise were drawn from skins, and the landscapes were probably based on A R Wallace's descriptions of his wanderings in the Malayan islands. Although Gould was an invalid in old age, he never lost interest in birds or in planning new books. Drawings by William Hart for a contemplated book on cassowaries were found after Gould's death in 1881 by Sotherans, the booksellers, who bought his estate. Had it been completed it would have added an impressive final chapter to the great ornithological achievements of John Gould.

THE PLATES

Plate 1

Plate 2

Plate 3

Plate 4

TRAGOPAN HASTINGSII
(Tor Toon)

Plate 5

22

Plate 6

BUCEROS CAVATUS.

Plate 7

Plate 8

Plate 9

Plate 10

PALÆORNIS NOVÆ-HOLLANDIÆ.

New Holland Parrakeet.

in the Possession of the Right Hon. the Countess of Mountcharles

1 Male 2 Female

PLYCTOLOPHUS ROSACEUS.

Plate 11

MACROCERCUS ARARAUNA.

Plate 12

MACROCERCUS ARACANGA.

Red and Yellow Macaw.

Plate 13

TROGON COLLARIS

Drawn from Nature & on Stone by J.& E. Gould.   Printed by C Hullmandel

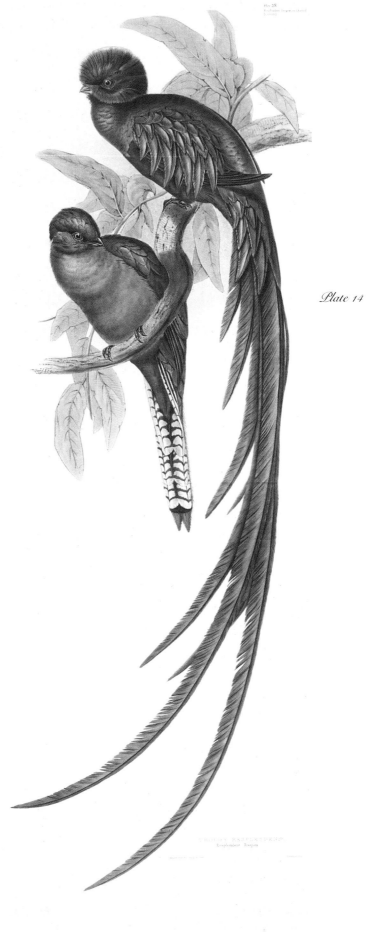

Plate 14

TROGON RESPLENDENS
Resplendent Trogon

PLATE 17

Plate 15

Plate 16

Ruby-throated Humming Bird. *No 1 & 2 Males 3*
"TROCHILUS POLLUBIS."
Plant Begonia odorata
Aylor Trumpet Flower.

Carolina Parrot. Males 1, F. 2, Young 3.
PSITTACUS CAROLINENSIS.
Plant Vulgo. Cuckle Burr.

Plate 17

Plate 18

PLATYCERCUS PENNANTII

Plate 19

Plate 20

Plate 21

Plate 22

Plate 23

Plate 24

Plate 25

Plate 26

Plate 27

Plate 28

Plate 29

Plate 30

Plate 31

Plate 32

Plate 33

Plate 34

Plate 35

Plate 36

CACATUA GYMNOPIS

Plate 37

Plate 38

Solomon Islands

Plate 39

Plate 40

LIST OF PLATES

Plate 1   Spotted Kingfisher *Alcedo guttatus* Lithograph J. and E. Gould
A Century of Birds from the Himalayas

Plate 2   Indian Magpie *Pica erythrorhyncha* Lithograph J. and E. Gould
A Century of Birds from the Himalayas

Plate 3   Satyr Tragopan *Tragopan satyra* Lithograph J. and E. Gould
A Century of Birds from the Himalayas

Plate 4   Hasting's Tragopan *Tragopan Hastingsii* Lithograph
J. and E. Gould *A Century of Birds from the Himalayas*

Plate 5   Impeyan Pheasant *Lophophorus Impeyanus* Lithograph
J. and E. Gould *A Century of Birds from the Himalayas*

Plate 6   Hornbill *Buceros cavatus* Lithograph
J. and E. Gould *A Century of Birds from the Himalayas*

Plate 7   Golden Thrush from Bengal Watercolour
George Edwards

Plate 8   Red-capped Parrakeet *Platycercus pileatus* Lithograph
Edward Lear *Family of Psittacidae or, Parrots*

Plate 9   Cockatiel *Nymphicus hollandicus* Lithograph
Edward Lear *Family of Psittacidae or Parrots*

Plate 10   Salmon-crested Cockatoo *Cacatua moluccensis* Lithograph
Edward Lear *Family of Psittacidae or, Parrots*

Plate 11   Blue and Yellow Maccaw *Macrocercus ararauna* Lithograph
Edward Lear *Family of Psittacidae or, Parrots*

Plate 12   Red and Yellow Maccaw *Macrocercus aracanga* Lithograph
            Edward Lear *Family of Psittacidae or, Parrots*

Plate 13   Collared Trogon *Trogon collaris* Lithograph J. and E. Gould
            Monograph of Trogons

Plate 14   Quetzal *Trogon resplendens* Lithograph J. and E. Gould
            Monograph of Trogons

Plate 15   Ruby-throated Humming-bird *Trochilus colubris* Aquatint
            J. J. Audubon *Birds of America*

Plate 16   Carolina Parrot *Psittacus carolinensis* Aquatint J. J. Audubon
            Birds of America

Plate 17   Crimson-rumped Toucanet *Aulacorhynchus haematopygus*
            Watercolour W. Hant

Plate 18   Pennant's Parrakeet *Platycerus Pennantii* Lithograph
            J. Gould & H. C. Richter *Birds of Australia*

Plate 19   Superb Lyre Bird *Menura superba* Lithograph J. and E. Gould
            Birds of Australia

Plate 20   Mrs. Gould's Sunbird *Cinnyris Gouldiae* Lithograph
            J. Gould & H. C. Richter *Birds of Asia*

Plate 21   Fiery Topaz *Topaz pyra* Lithograph J. Gould & H. C. Richter
            Family of Humming-birds

Plate 22   Chimborazian Hill-Star *Oreotrochilus chimborazo* Lithograph
            J. Gould & H. C. Richter *Family of Humming-birds*

Plate 23 Buffon's Plumeteer *Hypuroptila Buffoni* Lithograph

J. Gould & H. C. Richter *Family of Humming-birds*

Plate 24 Refulgent Wood-nymph *Thalurania refulgens* Lithograph

J. Gould & H. C. Richter *Family of Humming-birds*

Plate 25 Jacobin *Florisuga mellivora* Lithograph

J. Gould & H. C. Richter *Family of Humming-birds*

Plate 26 Ruby-throated Humming-bird *Trochilus colubris* Lithograph

J. Gould & H. C. Richter *Family of Humming-birds*

Plate 27 Floresi's Flamebearer *Selasphorus Floresii* Lithograph

J. Gould & H. C. Richter *Family of Humming-birds*

Plate 28 Marvellous Humming-bird *Loddigesia mirabilis* Lithograph

J. Gould & H. C. Richter *Family of Humming-birds*

Plate 29 Helena's Calypte *Calypte Helenae* Lithograph

J. Gould & H. C. Richter *Family of Humming-birds*

Plate 30 Shining Sunbeam *Aglaeactus cupreipennis* Lithograph

J. Gould & H. C. Richter *Family of Humming-birds*

Plate 31 Guerin's Helmet Crest *Oxypogon Guerini* Lithograph

J. Gould & H. C. Richter *Family of Humming-birds*

Plate 32 Golden-winged Bird of Paradise *Diphyllodes chrysoptera*

Lithograph W. Hart *Birds of New Guinea*

Plate 33 Count Raggi's Bird of Paradise *Paradisea Raggiana*

Lithograph W. Hart *Birds of New Guinea*

Plate 34   Papuan Bird of Paradise *Paradisea papuana* Lithograph

W. Hart *Birds of New Guinea*

Plate 35   Blue-eyed Cockatoo *Cacatua ophthalmica* Lithograph W. Hart

Birds of New Guinea

Plate 36   Naked-eyed Cockatoo *Cacatua gymnopis* Watercolour W. Hart

Birds of New Guinea

Plate 37   Solomon-Island Fruit-pigeon *Ptilopus solomonensis* Watercolour

W. Hart *Birds of New Guinea*

Plate 38   Richard's Fruit-pigeon *Ptilopus Richardsii* Watercolour

W. Hart *Birds of New Guinea*

Plate 39   Purple and Violet Manucode *Phonygama purpureo-violacea*

Watercolour W. Hart *Birds of New Guinea*

Plate 40   Two-wattled Cassowary *Casuarius bicarunculatus* Watercolour

W. Hart *Birds of New Guinea*